Your Amazing Body

Eyes

by Imogen Kingsley

Bullfrog Books

Ideas for Parents and Teachers

Bullfrog Books let children practice reading informational text at the earliest reading levels. Repetition, familiar words, and photo labels support early readers.

Before Reading
- Discuss the cover photo. What does it tell them?
- Look at the picture glossary together. Read and discuss the words.

Read the Book
- "Walk" through the book and look at the photos. Let the child ask questions. Point out the photo labels.
- Read the book to the child, or have him or her read independently.

After Reading
- Prompt the child to think more. Ask: What things do you enjoy looking at? What do you wish you didn't have to see at all?

Bullfrog Books are published by Jump!
5357 Penn Avenue South
Minneapolis, MN 55419
www.jumplibrary.com

Library of Congress Cataloging-in-Publication Data

Names: Kingsley, Imogen, author.
Title: Eyes / by Imogen Kingsley.
Description: Minneapolis, MN: Jump!, Inc. [2017]
Series: Your amazing body
"Bullfrog Books are published by Jump!"
Audience: Ages 5–8. | Audience: K to grade 3.
Includes bibliographical references and index.
Identifiers: LCCN 2016047280 (print)
LCCN 2016049075 (ebook)
ISBN 9781620316856 (hardcover: alk. paper)
ISBN 9781620317389 (pbk.)
ISBN 9781624965623 (ebook)
Subjects: LCSH: Eye—Juvenile literature.
Vision—Juvenile literature.
Classification: LCC QP475.7 .K5645 2017 (print)
LCC QP475.7 (ebook) | DDC 612.8/4—dc23
LC record available at https://lccn.loc.gov/2016047280

Editor: Jenny Fretland VanVoorst
Book Designer: Molly Ballanger
Photo Researcher: Molly Ballanger

Photo Credits: Alamy: Fumio Nabata/AFLO, 4, 5, 6–7. Getty: PeopleImages, 18; kirin_photo, 20–21. Shutterstock: Samuel Borges Photography, cover; szefei, 1; espies, 3; michaeliung, 8–9; mikeledray, 8–9; 3445128471, 10; Joseph Sohm, 11; altanaka, 12–13; Africa Studio, 14–15; Ben Schonewille, 16–17; Chinnapong, 16–17; Pair Srinrat, 16–17; OnlyZoia, 19; Tefi, 22; ivosar, 23tl; Tomsickova Tatyana, 23tr; Alex Mit, 23bl; IB Photography, 24.

Printed in the United States of America at Corporate Graphics in North Mankato, Minnesota.

Table of Contents

Look Out! 4

Parts of the Eye 22

Picture Glossary 23

Index 24

To Learn More 24

Look Out!

Look out!
A snowball!

4

Lin sees it.
She moves.

Eyes are amazing!

They get information.

They send it
to the brain.

Then we know
what we see.

We can see in color.

Wen sees a rainbow.

Dag watches a game.

snail

We can see close up.

Liam looks at a snail.

How do eyes work?
The pupil is black.
It lets in light.

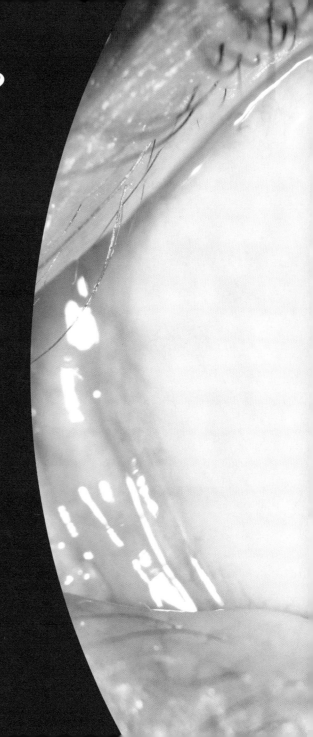

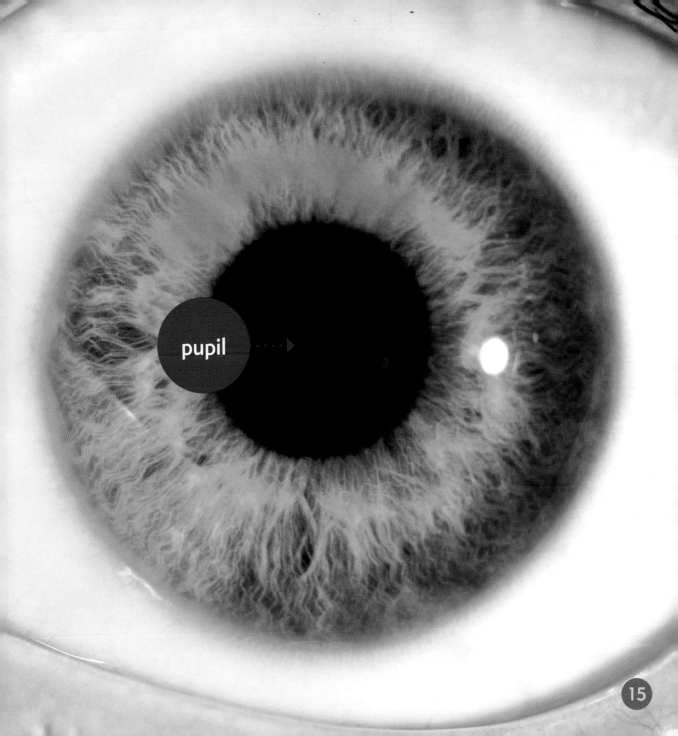

pupil

lens

16

The lens is clear.
It focuses light.

17

The retina has rods and cones.
They see colors.

They see shapes.

They make messages to send to the brain.

19

Look around you.

Look closely.

What do you see?

Parts of the Eye

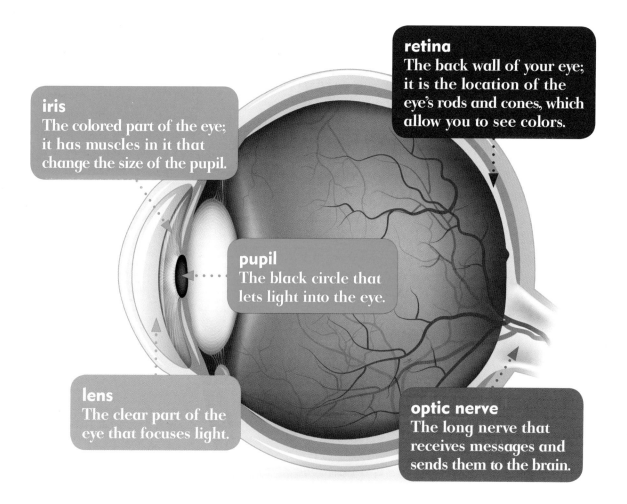

retina
The back wall of your eye; it is the location of the eye's rods and cones, which allow you to see colors.

iris
The colored part of the eye; it has muscles in it that change the size of the pupil.

pupil
The black circle that lets light into the eye.

lens
The clear part of the eye that focuses light.

optic nerve
The long nerve that receives messages and sends them to the brain.

Picture Glossary

brain
The "message center" part of your body.

rainbow
An arc of different colors that occurs when sunlight shines through a mist.

clear
See-through.

snail
A small animal with no legs, a soft, slimy body, and a shell on its back.

Index

brain 7, 19

clear 17

close 13

color 8, 18

far 10

information 7

lens 17

light 14, 17

messages 19

pupil 14

retina 18

rods and cones 18

To Learn More

Learning more is as easy as 1, 2, 3.

1) Go to www.factsurfer.com

2) Enter "eyes" into the search box.

3) Click the "Surf" button to see a list of websites.

With factsurfer.com, finding more information is just a click away.